# UNDERSTANDING
# ALCOHOL

## UPFRONT HEALTH

Published in the United States of America by Cherry Lake Publishing
Ann Arbor, Michigan
www.cherrylakepublishing.com

Reading Adviser: Marla Conn MS, Ed., Literacy specialist, Read-Ability, Inc.

Photo Credits: ©Prakasit Khuansuwan/EyeEm/Getty Images, cover; ©Alex Tihonovs/EyeEm/
Getty Images, 1; ©Jean-Philippe Tournut/Getty Images, 5; ©lisafx/Getty Images, 9; ©Traitov/
Getty Images, 10; ©sturti/Getty Images, 15; ©Milkos/Getty Images, 19; ©Ghislain & Marie
David de Lossy/Getty Images, 21; ©India Picture/Shutterstock, 23; ©Dan Dalton/Getty
Images, 25; ©Utah-based Photographer Ryan Houston/Getty Images, 27; ©pixelheadphoto
digitalskillet/Shutterstock, 29; ©lisafx/Getty Images, 30

Library of Congress Cataloging-in-Publication Data has been filed and is available
at catalog.loc.gov

Cherry Lake Publishing would like to acknowledge the work of The Partnership for 21st
Century Learning.
Please visit *www.p21.org* for more information.

Printed in the United States of America
Corporate Graphics

## ABOUT THE AUTHOR

Renae Gilles is an author, editor, and ecologist from the Pacific Northwest. She has a
bachelor's degree in humanities from Evergreen State College and a master's in biology
from Eastern Washington University. Renae and her husband currently live in the
Northeast with their two daughters, dog, and flock of backyard chickens.

# TABLE OF CONTENTS

# CHAPTER 1

# The World of Alcohol

Alcohol is important to many cultures around the world. People drink alcohol at social events and celebrations. Alcohol is served at restaurants, concerts, and sports games. It can be seen in ads, movies, TV shows, and online. Alcohol can be found almost everywhere, but it is a **drug**. A small amount relaxes the body and mind. A large amount can cause great harm. It can lead to injury, brain damage, and death.

Alcohol is made through **fermentation**. Water is mixed with something that contains sugars. Fruit, grain, or honey can be used. Tiny organisms, called yeast, eat the sugars. The yeast then creates **ethyl alcohol**. Unlike other types of food and drink, ethyl alcohol has a strong effect on the body.

Ancient winemakers would give their best products to their leaders as gifts.

Alcohol is a very ancient drink. Throughout history, beer has been like a food item. Scientists found beer from 10,000 years ago. Ancient Chinese, Egyptian, Greek, and Roman people enjoyed alcohol. During the Middle Ages, religious people called monks made beer and wine. Alcohol has also been used in medicine. It is a part of some people's religions. Many people have made it at home. This includes George Washington, the first president of the United States.

# The End of Prohibition

*Alcohol* **prohibition** *ended in the United States in 1933. A law made it legal again to make, drink, and sell alcohol. It also gave each state the right to make its own laws about drinking. Some places made rules about where and when people could buy alcohol. Others stayed* **dry**. *Many dry places have started to change their rules. For example, more than 22 counties and 200 cities in Texas began allowing alcohol sales in 2000. Why do you think these places are changing their laws? What might be the impact of the changes?*

In the early 1900s, people started to question drinking. They blamed alcohol for many problems in society. Many countries in Europe and North America went through a time of prohibition. This included the United States.

Today, drinking is common. About 86 percent of adults in the United States have tried alcohol. More than half of American adults drink at least once a month. Most of these people drink to relax and socialize. Many make or drink alcohol as a hobby. However, drinking becomes a problem for some people.

Drinking too much ethyl alcohol affects people's brains. It makes them lose control of their actions. Some people get alcohol use disorder (AUD). AUD is a brain disease. It means someone has no control of their drinking. They feel depressed without it. About 6 percent of adults in the United States have had AUD at some point in their lives. Out of these people, less than 10 percent get help.

## Abstinence versus Moderation

*Students have been taught about alcohol in school since the 1800s. In modern times, schools have focused on* **abstinence***. They teach about the dangers of drinking. Students are told to not try alcohol until they are adults. Scientists have shown that abstinence education does not work well. Some people suggest that schools focus on* **moderation** *instead. These programs admit that some students might decide to try alcohol. They teach students how to make safe choices if they do decide to drink. How are these programs similar? How are they different? Which do you think would work best?*

# The Effects of Alcohol

Alcohol can have many different effects on a person. It mostly depends on how much a person drinks and what they are drinking. Beer contains the least amount of alcohol. Beer is usually around 5 percent alcohol. That means it is 95 percent water and 5 percent ethyl alcohol. Wine is about 12 percent alcohol. Liquor is much stronger. Liquor is about 40 percent. In the United States, one drink means one can of beer (12 ounces), one glass of wine (5 ounces), or one shot of liquor (1.5 ounces).

Police officers conduct field sobriety tests to help determine if a driver has been drinking too much to drive.

The ethyl alcohol in a drink is absorbed by the stomach and small intestine. It enters the bloodstream. The heart then pumps the blood to the brain. A small amount of alcohol makes a person feel loose and relaxed. It also reduces their coordination, reflexes, and reaction times. Then the liver breaks down the ethyl alcohol. The effects wear off. For the average adult, this happens with one drink in one hour. That is considered normal alcohol use.

After heavy drinking, many people experience headaches, nausea, weakness, and other symptoms.

If someone drinks large amounts of alcohol very quickly, the liver cannot keep up. The effects on the brain are stronger. This is when someone becomes "drunk," or alcohol-**impaired**. People start to slur their speech. They get very emotional. They can become very happy, sad, or angry. They lose all coordination. Eyesight is also affected. A very large amount of alcohol can lead to vomiting, unconsciousness, and even a coma. This is considered alcohol **abuse**. Long-term alcohol abuse damages the brain. Communication and motor skills become more difficult. The heart is weakened.

# Alcohol Impairment Chart

## Men
### *Approximate Blood Alcohol Percentage*

| Drinks | Body Weight in Pounds | | | | | | | | |
|--------|------|------|------|------|------|------|------|------|---|
| | 100 | 120 | 140 | 160 | 180 | 200 | 220 | 240 | |
| 0 | .00 | .00 | .00 | .00. | .00 | .00 | .00 | .00 | **Only Safe Driving Limit** |
| 1 | .04 | .03 | .03 | .02 | .02 | .02 | .02 | .02 | **Impairment Begins** |
| 2 | .08 | .06 | .05 | .05 | .04 | .04 | .03 | .03 | **Driving Skills Affected** Possible Criminal Penalties |
| 3 | .11 | .09 | .08 | .07 | .06 | .06 | .05 | .05 | |
| 4 | .15 | .12 | .11 | .09 | .08 | .08 | .07 | .06 | |
| 5 | .19 | .16 | .13 | .12 | .11 | .09 | .09 | .08 | |
| 6 | .23 | .19 | .16 | .14 | .13 | .11 | .10 | .09 | |
| 7 | .26 | .22 | .19 | .16 | .15 | .13 | .12 | .11 | **Legally Intoxicated** |
| 8 | .30 | .25 | .21 | .19 | .17 | .15 | .14 | .13 | |
| 9 | .34 | .28 | .24 | .21 | .19 | .17 | .15 | .14 | **Criminal Penalties** |
| 10 | .38 | .31 | .27 | .23 | .21 | .19 | .17 | .16 | |

## Women
### *Approximate Blood Alcohol Percentage*

| Drinks | Body Weight in Pounds | | | | | | | | | |
|--------|-----|------|------|------|------|------|------|------|------|---|
| | 90 | 100 | 120 | 140 | 160 | 180 | 200 | 220 | 240 | |
| 0 | .00 | .00 | .00 | .00. | .00 | .00 | .00 | .00 | .00 | **Only Safe Driving Limit** |
| 1 | .05 | .05 | .04 | .03 | .03 | .03 | .02 | .02 | .02 | **Impairment Begins** |
| 2 | .10 | .09 | .08 | .07 | .06 | .05 | .05 | .04 | .04 | **Driving Skills Affected** Possible Criminal Penalties |
| 3 | .15 | .14 | .11 | .10 | .09 | .06 | .07 | .06 | .06 | |
| 4 | .20 | .18 | .15 | .13 | .11 | .10 | .09 | .06 | .06 | |
| 5 | .25 | .23 | .19 | .16 | .14 | .13 | .11 | .10 | .09 | |
| 6 | .30 | .27 | .23 | .19 | .17 | .15 | .14 | .12 | .11 | |
| 7 | .35 | .32 | .27 | .23 | .20 | .18 | .16 | .14 | .13 | **Legally Intoxicated** |
| 8 | .40 | .36 | .30 | .26 | .23 | .20 | .18 | .17 | .15 | |
| 9 | .45 | .41 | .34 | .29 | .26 | .23 | .20 | .19 | .17 | **Criminal Penalties** |
| 10 | .51 | .45 | .38 | .32 | .28 | .25 | .23 | .21 | .19 | |

## Driving Under the Influence

*One of the most dangerous things an alcohol-impaired person can do is drive. Even a small amount of alcohol affects coordination and reaction times. When behind the wheel of a 4,000-pound vehicle, it can be deadly. There have been many efforts to stop drinking and driving. Commercials share horror stories. Police set up checkpoints. Devices stop drunk people from starting cars. Still, almost 30 percent of deaths related to driving are due to alcohol. Can you think of other ways to solve this problem? Brainstorm a list of other methods. Be sure to include creative solutions.*

The liver can stop working. The **pancreas** can develop serious problems.

Alcohol doesn't just harm a person's body. It can harm their social lives. When drinking, many people embarrass themselves. They might act foolishly, make poor decisions, or vomit on themselves. They might get in fights with their friends. A drunk person might say or post things online that haunt them forever.

[ 21ST CENTURY SKILLS LIBRARY ]

# Social Media and Drinking

*In the 21st century, **social media** is everywhere. Anything a person says or does can end up online. This includes anything they say or do while drinking. There have been many times when one tweet or photo has changed someone's life. People have been expelled from school. Bosses have fired employees. Others have decided to not hire someone after seeing photos or posts about drinking. In most cases, this is legal. Schools and private businesses can make decisions after seeing social media. Many people think it is unfair. What is your opinion? Social media can also be used in a positive way. People can showcase their talents and skills for potential employers. What are some ways you could use social media in a positive way?*

# CHAPTER 3

# Teen Drinking

Alcohol abuse affects teens differently than adults. A teenager's body is still growing. If they abuse alcohol, their brains, organs, muscles, and bones may not grow properly. As an adult, they may have trouble with memory and learning. They might struggle with motor skills and coordination. This can make it more difficult to go to college, get a job, and do normal day-to-day activities. There is a very strong link between drinking as a teen and developing AUD as an adult. Teens who **binge drink** are more likely to have bad grades. They get in trouble with the law. They are more likely to try other drugs and make poor choices when it comes to sex.

Drinking games can quickly lead to the overconsumption of alcohol.

Even though alcohol is dangerous, many teens decide to try it. Drinking is a personal decision. Each person's reasons are different. A teen may try alcohol to relieve stress or depression. Teens may drink for social reasons. They see drinking in ads or at home. Then they think it's okay for them to try. Often, teens try alcohol simply because they are bored. Teens also have an urge to take risks. They have a need to try new things. This is completely normal. But alcohol is never a safe outlet.

## Drinking Laws Around the World

*Different countries have different laws for when people can start drinking. In most countries, the age limit is 18 or 19 years old. This includes most of Europe and South America. The United States is one of only 12 countries with an age limit of 21 years. In 2016, researchers asked teens between 15 and 19 years old if they had drunk heavily in the past 30 days. In the United States, 28 percent said yes. In Canada, 22.4 percent said yes. In the United Kingdom, it was 32.6 percent; France, 35.5; Germany, 39.5; and Russia, 28.6. In South America, Argentina was at 22 percent and Brazil, 15. What conclusions can you draw from this information?*

Another reason behind teen drinking is **peer** pressure. Teens feel pressure differently than adults. Most adults don't care as much what others think about them. But many teenagers are very aware of their peers' opinions. When it comes to alcohol, there are two types of pressure. Direct social pressure is when someone is offered a drink. Other people may be watching. They may be teased for saying no.

Indirect pressure is when someone feels like they should drink just by being around it. No one is offering alcohol. No one is even paying attention. This type of pressure can be just as powerful. It is important for teenagers to think about the types of pressure they may be feeling.

## Advertising Alcohol

*In 2017, alcohol companies made about $72 billion in the United States. Each year, those companies spend millions of dollars on advertising. Scientists think middle school students see 2 to 4 alcohol ads a day. The ads are mostly on billboards, store signs, and TV. Young people who see more ads are more likely to think drinking will be fun. Advertisers create this idea on purpose. They use music, humor, or animal characters. When coming across alcohol ads, it is important to stop and think. You can ask yourself questions. How is this ad trying to get my attention? How does it make me feel? How has it changed my thinking? What else do I know about this topic? Who created this ad? What is the purpose of this ad?*

# CHAPTER 4

# Solving Alcohol Use Disorder

Alcohol abuse can lead to alcohol use disorder. When a person drinks large amounts of alcohol regularly, it changes their brain. The brain becomes **dependent** on the alcohol. It is possible to recover from AUD, but it is not easy. Many people with AUD fight it all their lives.

The first step to recovery is to get help. This starts with talking to someone. It can be a parent or other family member. Or it can be a guidance counselor or teacher. The conversation needs to feel safe and comfortable. Sometimes people do not feel comfortable talking to someone they know. They can find information in books or online first. There are also hotlines that they can call for advice. The Substance Abuse and Mental Health Services Administration (SAMHSA) can be reached at

Recovery from AUD requires commitment, honesty, and support.

1-800-662-HELP (4357). This type of support is free and confidential.

People with AUD are usually helped at a **treatment** center. It may be a private business or a government program. While there, the person often stops drinking for the first time. Their bodies are dependent on alcohol. They go through **withdrawal**. People going through the early days of abstinence are very fragile. They need a lot of support. Professional counselors provide help and education. They share tools for leading a life without drinking.

## How to Treat AUD

*Professionals around the world have different opinions on AUD treatment. Some people believe medications are best. Pills can stop the brain from wanting alcohol. Or they can make people feel sick if they drink. Other professionals think* **behavioral** *treatment is best. People are taught to focus on controlling their thoughts and actions. Certain behavioral methods have people do it on their own. Others use the help of family and community members. Alternative treatments are also on the rise. These can include yoga, meditation, nutritional education, and art therapy. In what ways are these treatments different? How might they be the same?*

After treatment, someone with AUD may still struggle. They might think about alcohol and have urges to drink. Seeing alcohol in ads and movies or being around other people who are drinking can be difficult. Many people find being part of a group helps. Alcoholics Anonymous (AA) holds meetings across the country. A special group called Teen Addiction Anonymous (TAA) is just for teenagers. In these groups, people share their stories. They share ways to help maintain recovery.

More than 2 million people are members of Alcoholics Anonymous.

## Know the Signs

There are many warning signs of AUD. People at risk for AUD lose control of their drinking. They drink more or for longer periods of time than they planned. They try to quit or drink less, but cannot. Problem drinkers start to build up **tolerance** to alcohol. They may suffer from memory loss or mood swings. People at risk for AUD start to choose drinking over other things they like to do. They drink even if it causes problems with friends, family, work, school, or the law. It is important to be honest and aware of yourself and other people in your life. If you think you or a loved one might have a problem, reach out for help.

Some people recover from AUD completely. The majority of people do not. Even with professional treatment and support groups, more than 50 percent of people with AUD start drinking again.

People who overcome hardship in their life are
often more resilient in the long run.

# Making Healthy Choices

Everyone must make a decision about when they first try alcohol. Only you can make decisions for yourself. You will always have to live with the consequences of your decisions. Your decisions also affect those around you. This includes your family, your friends, and your community. Think about the people in your life now. Think about the people who might be a part of your future too.

Many people choose to follow alcohol abstinence. Many other people choose to drink to excess. Some of them never fully recover. Many people who choose to drink do it safely. They drink in safe environments, with people they know and trust. They avoid binge drinking and never drink and drive. They know their limit and know how to say "no" to both direct

The majority of adults drink very little alcohol. About 35 percent of American adults do not drink at all.

social pressure and indirect pressure.

Teenagers may choose to drink because they are stressed or depressed. There are better ways to fix these problems. Healthy food choices and regular physical activity are essential. This doesn't have to mean hitting the gym three days a week. Activities such as dancing, hiking, and swimming for fun are options too. Creating a relaxing environment for yourself is important. This means turning off the TV and smartphone. Learn to be quiet and calm without distraction. Journaling can also be a helpful way to work through bad feelings.

When bored and full of energy, there are ways to channel that energy in a healthy way. This can be done creatively. Try painting or making music. Or it can be done physically. Try playing sports or learning to rock climb. Join a club, take up a new hobby, or try out for a school play.

## Learning How to Say "No"

*Many teenagers end up around people who are drinking. This can happen even if they are trying to avoid it. There are many ways to say "no." You can be honest about your decision not to drink. You can say, "No thanks, I'm not into that." Or, "No, I'm going to wait." Coming up with an excuse such as "No, I'm not feeling very good" or "I have something important to do later" can work well. An offer of alcohol can also be ignored. It is perfectly fine to just walk away.*

Regular exercise helps a teenager maintain clear skin, grow stronger muscles and bones, get more sleep, and have better moods.

When making decisions about drinking, it is important to think about the effects of alcohol on the body and mind. It is important to know about the dangers and consequences of drinking. It is also important to think about your future. What are your goals? How might they be affected by alcohol abuse?

## Choosing Not to Drink

*A decision to not drink can be a difficult one. You might have to skip social events. You might stop being friends with some people. This is when a role model can be helpful. A role model is someone you look up to. You use them as an example for how you want to act. They can be a person in your life, such as a peer or important adult. Or it can be a famous person from the past or the present. With a strong role model behind you, you too can become a role model to your peers and those younger than you. Who are some of the role models in your life?*

Alcohol can interfere with graduating from college. About 30 percent of dropouts are due to problems with drinking.

# Think About It

Drinking and driving has been an issue for more than 100 years in the United States. The first Ford Model T went to market in 1908. The first law against drinking and driving was made two years later.

Today laws limit the amount of alcohol a driver can have in their system. Laws are in place at the national and state level. Laws aim to discourage people from drinking and driving, and to catch and punish those who do.

Using the internet and your local library, research the history of laws about drinking and driving. How have the laws changed? What people or events have influenced the changes?

# Learn More

## BOOKS

Bertovich, Yvonne. *Story of the Eighteenth Amendment and Prohibition, 100 Years Later*. Events That Changed the Course of History. Ocala, FL: Atlantic Publishing Group, Inc., 2017.

Bow, James. *Binge Drinking*. Talk Straight About . . . New York: Crabtree Publishing Company, 2015.

Covey, Sean. *Six Most Important Decisions You'll Ever Make: A Guide for Teens*. New York: Touchstone, 2017.

Doeden, Matt. *Health Smarts: How to Eat Right, Stay Fit, Make Positive Choices, and More*. Minneapolis: Twenty-First Century Books, 2013.

Krumsiek, Allison. *Teens and Alcohol: A Dangerous Combination*. Hot Topics. New York: Lucent, 2019.

## ON THE WEB

**Center for Media Literacy**
http://www.medialit.org/reading-room/five-key-questions-form-foundation-media-inquiry

**NIDA for Teens**
https://teens.drugabuse.gov/drug-facts/alcohol

**GirlsHealth**
https://www.girlshealth.gov/substance/alcohol/sayno.html

**MPOWRD**
https://www.mpowrd.org

# GLOSSARY

**abstinence (ab-STUH-nehnss)** the practice of avoiding thoughts or activities considered to be unhealthy

**abuse (uh-BYOOSS)** to misuse a substance in a way that harms the body

**behavioral (bee-HAYV-yer-uhl)** having to do with a person's actions and reactions

**binge drink (BINJ DREENK)** to drink a large amount of alcohol in a short amount of time

**dependent (dee-PEN-duhnt)** needing an outside source or substance to keep working

**drug (DRUG)** a substance that causes a chemical change in the body

**dry (DRIY)** not drinking or allowing alcohol

**ethyl alcohol (ETH-uhl AL-kuh-hahl)** a clear liquid used in adult beverages, medicine, and industry; also known as ethanol

**fermentation (fur-men-TAY-shun)** a chemical process during which yeasts and bacteria convert sugars into alcohol

**impaired (im-PAYRD)** unable to function in a normal or safe way

**moderation (MAH-dur-aye-shun)** the practice of avoiding excess and extremes in thoughts or activities

**pancreas (PAN-kree-uhss)** an organ in the body that helps digest food and regulate blood sugar

**peer (PEER)** someone who is in the same group, defined by age, rank, class, or skill, as another person

**prohibition (pro-hib-BISH-uhn)** the act of forbidding people from doing a certain action

**social media (SOH-shul MEE-dee-uh)** websites and applications through which people can communicate and share ideas using the internet

**tolerance (TALL-ehr-entz)** the ability to put up with something that is harmful or difficult

**treatment (TREET-muhnt)** a plan to help someone heal from a sickness or addiction, usually including medication or therapy

**withdrawal (WITH-drawl)** the painful and unpleasant physical reaction experienced when quitting drugs

# INDEX